WHOA! IT WORKS!

by Orlando Lopez

Don't forget your report

Modern Curriculum Press
Parsippany, New Jersey

Silly Putty® and Crayola® are registered trademarks of Binney & Smith Corporation.
Ivory® is a registered trademark of Procter & Gamble.
Frisbee® is a brand name and registered trademark of Mattel, Inc.
Post-it® is a registered trademark of 3M.
Slinky® is a registered trademark of James Industries.
Velcro® is a registered trademark of Velcro Industries B.V.
Popsicle® is a registered trademark of Good Humor-Breyers Ice Cream, Inc.

This book is not intended to be an endorsement or criticism of products
described herein.

Credits

Photos: All photos © Pearson Learning Group unless otherwise noted. Cover
Photography by: John Paul Endress for MCP. 10: *l.* F.J. Koster/Missouri Historical
Society; *r.* PhotoDisc, Inc. 11: Montague Lyon Collection/Missouri Historical Society.
15, 17: Courtesy of Binney & Smith Inc. 18: NASA. 19: Courtesy of Binney & Smith Inc.
20: Lewis Portnoy/The Stock Market. 21: Courtesy of Wham–O Inc. 22: UPI/Corbis-
Bettmann. 23: Courtesy of Wham–O Inc. 29: ©The Procter & Gamble Company, Used
by Permission. 30: ©Scott Camazine/Photo Researchers, Inc. 31: *t.* E.R.
Degginger/Color–Pic, Inc.; *b.* ©Dr. Jeremy Burgess/Science Photo Library/Photo
Researchers, Inc. 35, 37: *b.* Courtesy of 3M. 41, 42, 43: Courtesy of George
Greenwood. 45, 46, 47: Silver Burdett Ginn.

Cover and book design by Liz Kril

ISBN 0-7652-0887-3

Printed in the United States of America

11 12 13   07 06 05

Modern
Curriculum
Press

Pearson Learning Group

1-800-321-3106
www.pearsonlearning.com

Contents

For Mom, who loves gadgets and thingamajigs

An Inventor's Work

Plop! There goes your pencil again. Does your pencil always seem to roll off your desk no matter where you put it? What can you do about this problem? Invent something!

You might be thinking that you're not an inventor. Inventors think up big things like airplanes and computers. Think again!

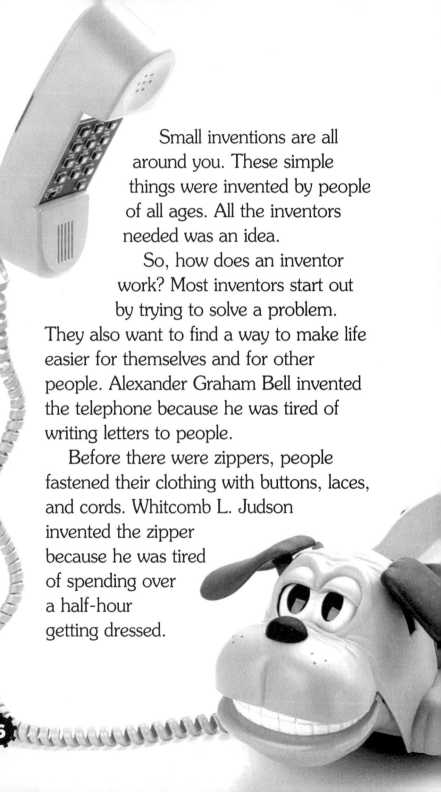

Small inventions are all around you. These simple things were invented by people of all ages. All the inventors needed was an idea.

So, how does an inventor work? Most inventors start out by trying to solve a problem. They also want to find a way to make life easier for themselves and for other people. Alexander Graham Bell invented the telephone because he was tired of writing letters to people.

Before there were zippers, people fastened their clothing with buttons, laces, and cords. Whitcomb L. Judson invented the zipper because he was tired of spending over a half-hour getting dressed.

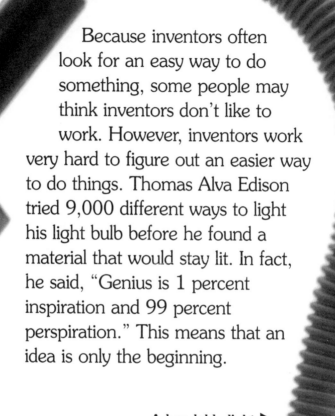

Because inventors often look for an easy way to do something, some people may think inventors don't like to work. However, inventors work very hard to figure out an easier way to do things. Thomas Alva Edison tried 9,000 different ways to light his light bulb before he found a material that would stay lit. In fact, he said, "Genius is 1 percent inspiration and 99 percent perspiration." This means that an idea is only the beginning.

A bendable light ▶

◀ A modern telephone

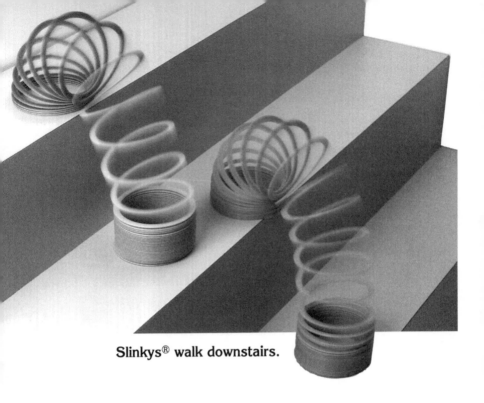

Slinkys® walk downstairs.

Some inventions were not planned. The inventor started out to invent one thing. Then he or she ended up inventing something else by accident.

The springy wire toy that can walk downstairs by itself was invented by accident. A man named Richard James worked on a Navy ship during World War II. One day a spring fell on a table. Then it flipped over and fell to the floor. James liked the way it moved. He thought it would make a fun toy.

James searched for a long time to find steel wire that would coil and uncoil in the right way. Finally, he found the right wire. Then, in 1945, he brought 400 Slinkys® to a store in Philadelphia. In just 90 minutes all 400 Slinkys were sold. The toy has been a big hit ever since.

NOTEBOOK INVENTOR'S NOTEBOOK

Richard James's wife, Betty, looked in a dictionary to find a name for the Slinky. She liked the word *slinky* because it meant "stealthy, sleek, and sinuous." Now in her 70s, Betty James still runs the Slinky company. The Slinkys are still made in the same shape as they were in 1945.

Chapter 2

Food Follies

Like many inventions, some foods were accidents. The accidents turned out to be something tasty that a lot of people wanted to eat.

The ice-cream cone was an accident. It solved a problem at the 1904 World's Fair. The fair was held in St. Louis, Missouri, during the summer. Summers in St. Louis are hot, so the ice-cream stands were very busy.

1904 World's Fair in St. Louis, Missouri

Children eating ice cream at the St. Louis World's Fair

One vendor was so busy that he ran out of dishes for his ice cream. Ernest A. Hamwi was selling his special waffles next to the ice-cream stand. When he saw there were no more dishes, he rolled a waffle into a cone shape. Then he put a scoop of ice cream inside. Everyone thought this was a great idea. The ice-cream cone was born.

Just after the ice-cream cone became a hit, the Popsicle® appeared one cold night. In 1905, a mix of soda-water powder and water was a popular drink. Eleven-year-old Frank Epperson mixed a drink one day. Then he put his drink with the stirring stick still in it on the back porch. He left it there all night. The next day, Frank found he had frozen soda water on a stick.

After Frank had grown up, he started a business making the frozen sticks in seven fruity flavors. He named the sticks Epsicles, after icicles and his own name, Epperson. Later, he changed the name to Popsicles.

Popsicles

An angry cook and a picky customer invented potato chips. In 1853, George Crum worked in the kitchen at the Carey Moon Lake House in Saratoga Springs, New York.

Crum tried hard to make his customers happy. One day a man kept sending his fried potatoes back to the kitchen. He wanted them thinner and cooked for a longer time.

Finally, Crum got angry. He made the potatoes as thin as possible. Then he fried them until they crisped and curled up. Just to make sure the customer hated them, Crum salted them well. Much to his surprise, the customer loved the potatoes. He even wanted more.

Potato chips

Soon everyone was talking about the crispy potatoes from Saratoga. They quickly became a favorite snack of millions of people. Today, many people still choose potato chips when they want a snack.

INVENTOR'S NOTEBOOK

NOTEBOOK

Some stories about accidental foods may or may not be true. How do you think doughnuts came to be? One story is that a sea captain needed both hands to steer. So he shoved the cake he had been eating over a spoke of the ship's steering wheel. Later he ate the cake. He thought it was much better with the soggy middle taken out.

Chapter 3

Full of Bounce

It bounces. It stretches. When laid flat on a newspaper, it picks up print and pictures. When hit with a hammer, it breaks like glass. What is this funny stuff? It's Silly Putty®!

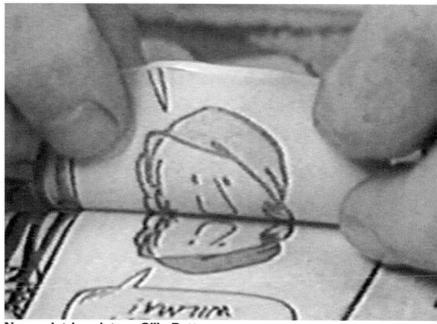

Newsprint imprint on Silly Putty

A Silly Putty egg

Silly Putty was an accident. It was created in 1944 in a company called General Electric. An engineer named James Wright was trying to invent a new material that could be used in place of rubber from trees. This material could then be used to make tires, boots, and other things.

Wright was working with silicone, a material that is made from sand. He tried one test in which he added boric acid to silicone oil. All of a sudden, he had gooey stuff that bounced.

A bouncing goo should be good for something, Wright thought. He sent the stuff to other engineers. No one could think of any good ideas.

Stretching Silly Putty

Then, in 1949, someone showed the bouncy goo to a man named Peter Hodgson. Hodgson had so much fun with it, he thought it should be a toy. So, he borrowed $147 to buy the goo from General Electric. He named it Silly Putty and sold it in plastic eggs.

After a few months, people started talking about the silly stuff. Suddenly, every kid in America had to have some Silly Putty. Soon, homes around the country had little pink balls of Silly Putty bouncing off the walls.

After Silly Putty had been around for awhile, people began to discover other ways to use the gooey stuff. They found out that it was great for cleaning typewriter keys and for getting lint off of clothing and pet hair off furniture. It was great for plugging leaks. It could also be put under a wobbly table leg.

Astronauts have taken Silly Putty into space. They used it to anchor tools in the weightlessness of space. They also played with it when they had nothing else to do.

Astronaut Tammy Jernigan plays around with Silly Putty.

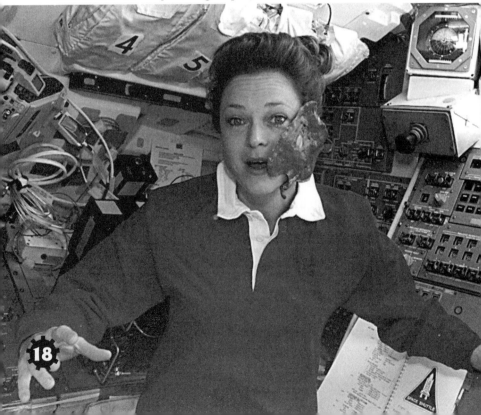

Silly Putty now comes in different forms and colors.

Other people have found that squeezing a ball of Silly Putty is a great way to make fingers and hands stronger. Playing with Silly Putty also helps some people to calm down.

Nearly 50 years after Silly Putty was first sold, the bouncy goo is still a hit with kids of all ages. And it's still silly!

INVENTOR'S
NOTEBOOK

Today, Silly Putty is made by Binney & Smith, Inc., the company that makes Crayola® crayons. It makes the putty in four bright colors. It also makes putty that glows in the dark.

Flying Pie Tins

Watch your head! A round, plastic disc comes flying across the lawn. Here comes a fast dog running after it. It leaps into the air and catches the disc.

Throwing a Frisbee® is a favorite sport of many people and dogs! Contests are held around America and in many other countries. There is even an International Frisbee Hall of Fame in Lake Linden, Michigan!

Dog catches Frisbee.

Frisbie's pie tins

The Frisbee did not start out as a toy. It was never supposed to be a flying disc, either. The Frisbee started out as a pie tin.

A baker in Connecticut, by the name of William Russell Frisbie, bought his own bakery in 1871. His sister baked pies and cookies. Frisbie traveled around selling them.

Each pie came in a special metal pie tin. It was ten inches wide. It had a raised edge, a big brim, and six little holes in the bottom. On the bottom were the words *Frisbie's Pies.*

Frisbie sold a lot of pies to students at Yale University. Soon, the baker noticed that the number of empty pie tins returned was less than the number of pies sold. He found that the students were keeping the tins. They liked to play catch with them. When they threw the heavy tins, they would yell "Frisbie!" Then people nearby would know to watch out for the flying discs.

People hoping to set a world record for tossing the most Frisbees into the air

Pluto Platter

The second part of the Frisbee invention started in 1948. At that time many Americans were interested in outer space. Lots of people liked to talk about flying saucers. A man named Walter Frederick Morrison decided he could make money on the outer-space craze. So he invented a flying-saucer toy.

At the same time, a material called plastic was invented. Morrison thought the new plastic would be great for his new toy. Finally, he found a kind of plastic that was soft, light, and strong. He called the model made in 1951 the Pluto Platter.

In 1955, Morrison met Richard Knerr and A. K. Melin. They were the owners of the Wham-O toy company. The men loved Morrison's flying disc. So, Morrison agreed to let them make and sell the Pluto Platter.

Knerr may have discovered the Frisbie name during a sales trip to Massachusetts. He may have heard Harvard students talking about the popular pie-tin game called "Frisbie-ing." Knerr would not have known how to spell Frisbie, but he probably thought it was a great name. So, the Pluto Platter became the Frisbee.

Another Wham-O worker, Ed Headrick, had another idea. He thought playing Frisbee could be a sport! A lot of other people thought so, too. They bought millions of Frisbees to use in contests.

Today, Frisbee is played everywhere. The game can even be played inside with Frisbees made of cloth and foam. Plastic Frisbees come in many colors. Some even have batteries and blinking lights. The Frisbee is still flying high.

INVENTOR'S NOTEBOOK

Fred Morrison wanted the people who played with his Pluto Platter to be inventors, too. He had the words *play catch, invent games, fly-flip away* put on one side of each flying disc.

The Soap That Floats

What happens when you drop a bar of soap in a bathtub or a sink full of water? Most bars sink, making them hard to find in the soapy water. If you are using Ivory® soap, however, you don't have to worry. That's because Ivory soap floats!

Ivory soap was not invented by someone who had a good idea for solving a problem of lost soap. It was invented by someone who made a big mistake.

In 1878, a worker at the Procter & Gamble Company was mixing soap. That year the company had started making a pure white soap they called White Soap.

The worker noticed it was just about time for lunch. He did not think he would be gone long. So, he left the soap-mixing machine running.

When he finally got back, the worker saw that the machine had been running for too long. A lot of air had been mixed into the soap. He thought the extra air would not hurt the soap. So, he went ahead and made the soap into bars. The bars were put in packages and shipped to stores.

Ivory® soap can fix sticky zippers and drawers.

In a few weeks the company began getting lots of letters. People wanted more of the soap that floated. It was then the company owners found out about the mistake. It turned out to be a wonderful mistake. The company had accidentally discovered a new kind of soap. It sold much better than their old soap!

Since then, people have found that Ivory soap can be rubbed on zippers to make them work more smoothly. It is also good for helping drawers and windows open and shut easily. Even itchy insect bites will feel better if rubbed with a wet bar of Ivory soap.

In the 1920s, Ivory soap became artistic. A company that wrote ads to sell Ivory soap had a contest to see who could carve the best statue from a bar of Ivory. The National Soap Sculpture Competition became a popular event.

Since Ivory soap was invented, over 30 billion bars have been made. That's a lot of floating soap!

Ivory soap carving

NOTEBOOK

INVENTOR'S
NOTEBOOK

Some people tell a somewhat different story about Ivory soap. They say the worker fell asleep. When he found his mistake, he threw the batch of soap into a nearby stream. He was surprised when his mistake floated away!

Chapter 6

A Sticky Problem

Have you ever gone for a walk in a field and come home with little plant burrs stuck to your pants and socks? It's not easy to pull them off. You may have wondered what makes those burrs so sticky.

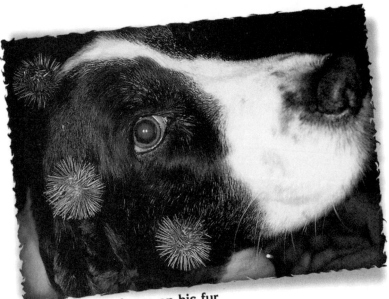

Dog with plant burrs on his fur

A Swiss engineer named George de Mestral wondered, too. He had gone for a walk with his dog one day in 1948. When they returned, he found his dog covered with cockleburs. Many of them were stuck to de Mestral's jacket and pants as well.

Instead of just pulling off the burrs and throwing them away, de Mestral decided to keep one. He put it under a microscope to take a closer look.

Burrs

When de Mestral looked through the microscope, he saw the burr was covered with tiny hooks.

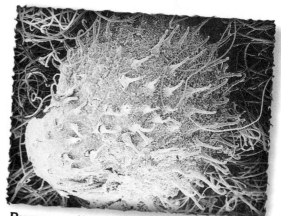

Burr magnified to show the hooks

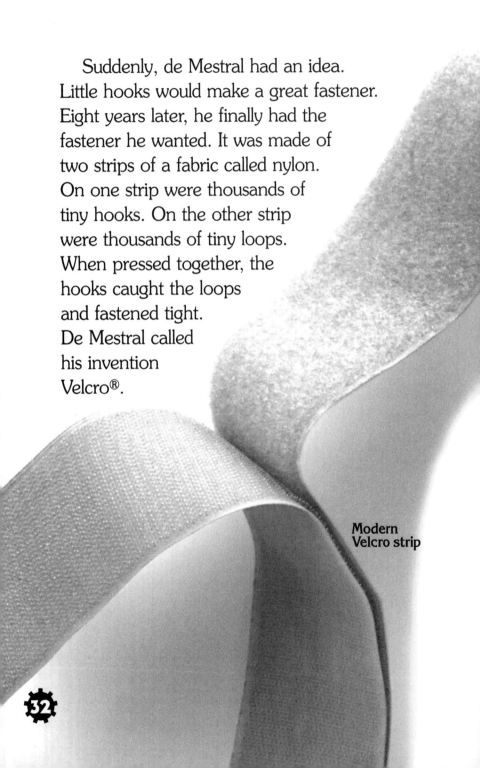

Suddenly, de Mestral had an idea.
Little hooks would make a great fastener.
Eight years later, he finally had the
fastener he wanted. It was made of
two strips of a fabric called nylon.
On one strip were thousands of
tiny hooks. On the other strip
were thousands of tiny loops.
When pressed together, the
hooks caught the loops
and fastened tight.
De Mestral called
his invention
Velcro®.

**Modern
Velcro strip**

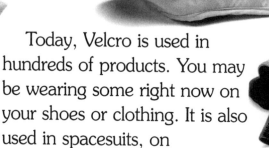

Velcro products include a dog coat, shoe straps, and a bicycle helmet.

Bogey

Today, Velcro is used in hundreds of products. You may be wearing some right now on your shoes or clothing. It is also used in spacesuits, on backpacks, watchbands, and in hospitals. You can use Velcro to hang pictures and other items. The possible uses for Velcro go on and on.

What a lucky accident it was when George de Mestral decided not to throw away that sticky burr!

NOTEBOOK

INVENTOR'S NOTEBOOK

Sometimes a new invention will cause problems for other inventions. When Velcro was invented, the companies that made zippers, snaps, buttons, and shoelaces lost business.

Chapter 7

Post a Note Anywhere

Art Fry had a problem. One Sunday in 1970, he tried to mark with bits of paper the songs he would be singing with his church choir. By the time the second church service started, some of the markers had fallen to the floor. Fry lost his place.

If only he could find a bookmark that would stick for just a little while! Then he could take it off without tearing the pages.

Paper bookmarks falling out of a book

Art Fry

Spencer Silver

Fry was a scientist at 3M, a company in St. Paul, Minnesota, that makes things like glue and tape. He remembered that a coworker, Spencer Silver, had tried to make a super-strong glue a few years before. Instead of being super strong, Spencer's glue turned out to be super weak. No one knew what to do with a glue that wouldn't hold things together. So, it was put in a storage room and forgotten.

Fry ordered some of Spencer's glue. He put it on paper markers and stuck the markers in books. The markers stayed in place and came off without tearing the pages. Fry knew he had a good idea.

It took Fry seven years to get 3M to see how wonderful Post-it® notes were. "Why would people want to pay for scratch paper?" his boss asked.

Finally, Fry wrote a question to his boss on a Post-it note and stuck it onto some other papers. His boss answered the question on the same Post-it note and sent it back to Fry. Later they realized they had more than a bookmark or scratch paper. They had a new way to communicate!

Until people used a Post-it note, they didn't know they needed one. But almost everyone who tried the notes wanted more. People loved the fun little sticky papers that could mark a book, send a note, and be stuck on a wall, phone, computer screen, chairs, or even clothing! The same note could easily be moved around and still stick.

Art Fry working in his laboratory

In just 15 years, Post-it notes became one of America's five top-selling office supply products. Post-its also became popular in homes and schools.

Post-it notes are now known all over the world. Art Fry and Spencer Silver are even in the National Museum of American History at the Smithsonian Institution in Washington, D.C.

Today, Post-it notes are made in 18 different colors, 27 different sizes, and 56 different shapes. The largest Post-it note is over 30 inches long. That's a little less than a yard long! The smallest note is one-half inch by two inches.

Post-it notes also come in different scents, such as bubble gum, chocolate, dill pickles, and pizza. No matter what their shape or scent, Post-it notes mark the spot and make sure the message gets through.

INVENTOR'S NOTEBOOK

Many people send 3M amazing stories about Post-it notes. One woman wrote that a Post-it note rode 3,000 miles stuck to the back of a rented trailer when her family moved from California to Kentucky.

Chapter 8

Toasty Ears

If your ears got very cold in the winter, what would you invent to keep them warm? Chester Greenwood's cold ears were a big problem. So he invented earmuffs!

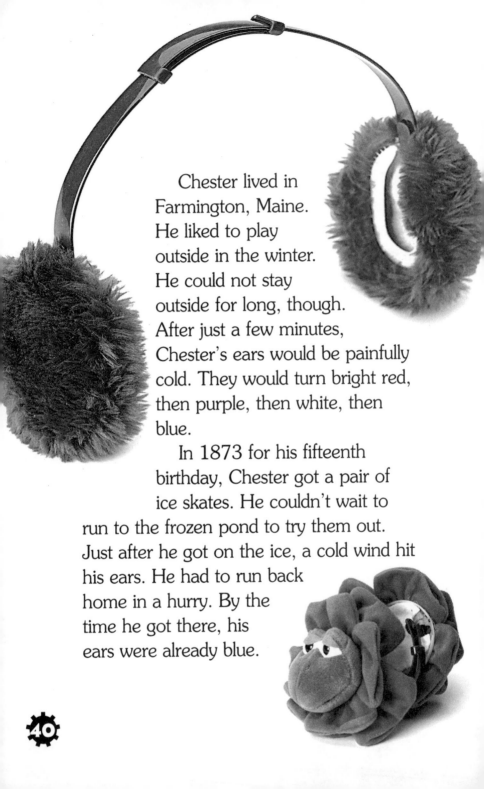

Chester lived in
Farmington, Maine.
He liked to play
outside in the winter.
He could not stay
outside for long, though.
After just a few minutes,
Chester's ears would be painfully
cold. They would turn bright red,
then purple, then white, then
blue.

In 1873 for his fifteenth
birthday, Chester got a pair of
ice skates. He couldn't wait to
run to the frozen pond to try them out.
Just after he got on the ice, a cold wind hit
his ears. He had to run back
home in a hurry. By the
time he got there, his
ears were already blue.

The next day he wrapped a heavy wool scarf around his head. His ears were finally warm. But the scarf was very scratchy. He had to turn around and go home again.

On the third day, Chester tried again. This time he made loops out of wire. Then he asked his grandmother to sew a piece of beaver fur on one side of each loop. On the other side of the fur, she sewed a piece of black velvet. She then sewed the whole thing to Chester's cap.

Chester headed for the skating pond. His ears stayed warm and toasty the whole time he skated. He had solved his problem.

Chester's neighbors wanted warm ears, too. It wasn't long before Chester's mother and grandmother were busy bending wire and sewing ear covers.

Greenwood's Ear Protectors became a big money-making business. When Chester opened an earmuff factory, Farmington became the earmuff capital of the world.

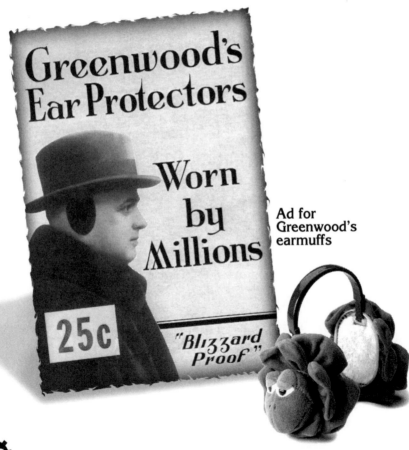

Ad for Greenwood's earmuffs

Old newspaper ad for earmuffs

Chester Greenwood invented many other things. However, he may be best known for his earmuffs. When he died, in 1937, his factory was making earmuffs 24 hours a day.

Earmuffs are still popular today. Cold ears everywhere are glad that Chester Greenwood had a good idea.

INVENTOR'S NOTEBOOK

Every winter a Chester Greenwood Day is held in Maine. Special events are held in Farmington. There is a parade and a coldest-ears contest.

Chapter 9

You Too Can Be an Inventor

As you can see, no idea is too small or too silly to become an invention. The next time you have a problem, think what you could invent to solve it. For example, do you remember the pencil that always rolled off the desk? How could you use Velcro or Silly Putty to solve that problem?

Timothy Shin, 9, of Northridge, California, was the second place primary winner in the 1998 Invention Convention. The convention is sponsored by science publisher, Silver Burdett Ginn. The invention is an automatic milk dispenser.

Inventors follow steps from an idea to a product. Here are some things to think about if you want to be an inventor.

Decide if you want to make money from your idea. If so, then you have to make your idea into an invention that people will buy.

Build your invention, or make a model. Then test it. You may have to build and test your model more than once to get it to work right.

Try not to use too many parts. Use simple materials, too. Your invention will cost less to make if you do.

Draw pictures and list materials for everything you make. Be willing to change your invention at any time to make it better.

Playing with a Hula Hoop®

When you have a model that works, try it out on other people. Find out what they think of it.

If your invention is a hit with your friends and family, you need a plan for making more.

You will also need to name your invention. Many names tell something about what the invention does. The name *Greenwood's Ear Protectors* told people what the invention would do for them.

Many names are fun. They make people wonder what your invention is and what they can do with it. For example, what would you do with a Hula Hoop?

After you have a product and a name, you need a way to sell your invention. An adult should help you with selling.

Elena Cucco, 8, (left) won first place in the primary division in the 1996 Invention Convention. She invented a Bunny Bottle Bonnet. Lizzie Gray, 11, (right) was the first place intermediate winner with her Flip-O-Matic music page turner.

There's a lot to think about when you're an inventor. It might help to talk to other people who have invented something. Each year there are invention conventions held in different places. At these events, inventors can show what they have created.

Being an inventor can be fun as well as hard work. Just remember one thing: Don't let anyone tell you, "That will never work!"

NOTEBOOK Inventor's NOTEBOOK

A patent says that an invention is registered with the U.S. government. The U.S. Patent and Trademark Office has given patents for some unusual inventions, such as a machine for patting a baby and an alarm clock that squirts water in a person's face.

47

Glossary

accident (AK suh dunt) an event that is not planned or expected

craze (krayz) an idea or item that everyone talks about or wants for a period of time

disc (dihsk) a thin, flat, round plate; also *disk*

genius (JEEN yus) a high mental ability

inspiration (ihn spur AY shun) something that causes a thought or an action that leads to something new

inventor (ihn VEN tur) a person who is the first to think about or make something new

microscope (MYE kruh skohp) a device or instrument that has a lens or group of lenses that make little things look larger so they can be studied

patent (PAT nt) the right given by a government saying that a person is the only one who can make and sell a certain invention

product (PRAHD ukt) an object or an idea that can be sold

vendor (VEN dur) a person who sells a product, such as drinks at a baseball game